MICROWAVE COOKING FOR ONE

MICROWAVE COOKING FOR ONE

Easy and Delicious Recipes for the Solo Cook

Yvonne Webb
with an introduction by
Ross Alexander

Bay Books
Sydney London

Acknowledgements

I am grateful to Sanyo for providing a Sanyo microwave oven for testing recipes and particularly to Coralanne Heathcote who made many helpful comments and suggestions in the development of the book. Thanks also to the C.S.I.R.O. Division of Food Research Information Service for permission to use material from their pamphlets 'The Nutritional Value of Processed Foods', 'The Storage Life of Foods' and 'Handling Food in the Home', and to the Indian Head Glass Container Group, U.S.A., for information on the use of glass in microwave cooking.

Thanks to all my friends who revived the flagging spirit. Special thanks go to: Ross who provided the inspiration and motivation for the book. Bill, Jerry and Ted who survived and enjoyed the recipes. Jan and Joy whose love of microwave potatoes produced the ideal recipe. Clients of the Q.I.T. Weight Control Clinic who enthusiastically provided ideas. Margaret whose exceptional patience and typing made the book a reality. Kerry and Greg who translate a plate of food into an art form.

Photography by Ashley Barber

Published in the UK by Angus & Robertson (UK) Ltd., 16 Golden Square, London. W1R 4BN

Publisher: George Barber

Copyright © Yvonne Webb 1984

National Library of Australia Card number and ISBN 0 85835 808 5

Designed by Gus Cohen

Typesetting by Savage Type Pty Ltd, Brisbane

The publisher would like to thank Voula Kyprianou for assistance in preparing dishes.

The publisher would like to thank the following for their assistance during the photographing of dishes for this book: The Bay Tree Kitchen Shop and David Jones (Aust) Pty Ltd (for cutlery and dinnerware); Sanyo and Westinghouse (for microwave ovens); and Fred Pazzoti Pty Ltd (for tiles).

CONTENTS

INTRODUCTION

The Solo Lifestyle

Going Solo is a mild challenge and potentially a lot of fun. If you've decided that a life of togetherness is not for you, have left your parents for a life on your own, or it is just the luck of the draw — great! This book is for you.

Living alone is a fine lifestyle. Seven days a week, apart from striking the necessary blows for profits, a Solo has only self satisfying schedules, moves at will, and is always quite free to invite someone home for a visit.

But a Solo's lifestyle really comes into its own when night falls and the weary ploughmen (and women) have plodded home. Solos are then free of the tyranny of the sun dial, the quartz watch, a live-in friend or a family. If the conversation is good, if the scene is pleasant, if a miracle might happen, if there's a new show in town — it's all up to the Solo. Go or stay.

Solos have a choice of every BYO in the city and of the better bars that put macadamia nuts near the wooden bowls of olives.

A Solo often heads for bed without so much as glancing at the cooking appliances collected to provide the easy, healthy snacks that never seem to materialise. Usually they are all in mint condition and there is little need to clean the pristine wall oven.

In many Solo kitchens soup tins in a cupboard and frozen food packs in the top section of the fridge impress the curious. Milk, marg, eggs, bread, soda, tonic, Coke, dry, champers, white burgundy and useful cans take up most of the working department of the electric Coolgardie safe.

But be honest. A Solo's life has its drawbacks.

These are cooking at home, missed meals, what is loosely called diet, and the fact that food preparation often involves the only sophisticated cooking gadget that Solos tend to master — the cast iron frypan. It means a certain sameness, but then you can always eat Chinese on the way home if it's not too late.

All this Solo's problems were solved by a chance meeting at a stop smoking seminar after speaking on the pleasures of chain smoking. There were comments on this Solo's lifestyle, not all good and none informed.

It led a healthy life enthusiast with a weakness for lost causes to research and write this book. It was done on the basis that if this Solo could prepare the recipes, anyone could, and probably would.

Solo, male or female, you now hold in your hand the answer to all our problems.

A microwave oven, a few table-worthy platters, some quick shopping where the scenery is good — then you've got your menu selection ready to go and all is only a few feet from the friendly home refrigerator.

You also get some fair enough general advice thrown in, although Solos are not noted for taking or seeking a lot of this.

You won't find a repeat of the recipes that come in the box with your microwave oven. In *Microwave Cooking for One* you'll find quick, unusual, with-it recipes for loners, that you can prepare, cook, serve and eat with an absolute minimum of fuss. Even with pleasure. Perhaps even with some smug satisfaction.

Microwave Cooking for One doesn't make cooking fun. It's just quick and easy cookery for one, with civilised results that look and taste great. And it's not a temperance book.

There is a trap. There always is. A few tryouts with this cookbook could lead you to consider recipes for two, ask someone to dinner, let the red breathe and light the candles in the dining room.

Watch it. It could be the beginning of the end of a good lifestyle.

Ross Alexander

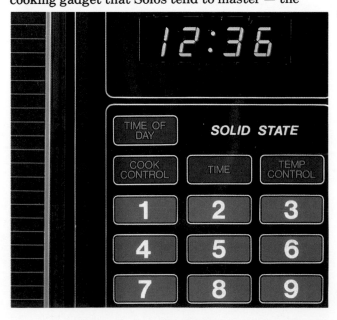

WHAT'S IT ALL ABOUT?

How to use this book

This book is intended as a sort of culinary survival guide for the person living alone who has few of the basic skills of cooking. Armed with it and your microwave oven (a boon to the Solo) a typical scenario might run like this.

You get home. You are starving and you need a meal in a hurry. No time for washing messy pans. Choose your recipe according to what's in the pantry. Put it all in the microwave oven. Put your face under cold water to revive, throw your shoes off, and your meal is ready.

While providing mostly very basic recipes, a few unusual and interesting touches have been added to stimulate an interest in food and cooking. Good nutrition, on which this book is based, means a variety of foods from each of these basic food groups every day:

1. fruit and vegetables
2. bread and cereals
3. milk and dairy products
4. meat, fish and eggs

A meal should be looked at in total and should be nutritionally balanced. A look into cupboard and fridge is the first step. Then plan the meal around what you find. The recipes are designed to be flexible; if cooked white meat is listed as an ingredient, then any cooked white meat will do. A slice of bread and cheese will pad out a fairly meagre meal. Remember good crusty bread is a nutritious and filling food.

This book does not propose to be a treatise on microwave cooking or housekeeping. A few ideas have been thrown together to give you confidence in nutritional food preparation using your microwave oven, so there are no very difficult or complicated recipes. Those can be found in any standard cookbook accompanying a microwave oven. Complicated recipes for dishes requiring slow cooking to bring out flavour are really not suitable for the type of microwave cooking this book is concerned with. Cooking times given are approximate and are designed to produce crispy vegetables. If a softer consistency is preferred, extra cooking time should be allowed. Each brand and type of microwave is slightly different and cooking times may vary by a minute or so, depending on your oven.

No precise measuring aids such as scales are required but when starting off cooking for one, it is a good idea to use standard sets of cups and spoons to become familiar with quantities used. Although exact measures are usually given, a little less or a little more of most ingredients will do just as well.

Ingredients lists have been kept short and herbs and spices are generally optional, but nice. Salt, pepper and sugar are only occasionally listed. However, to the addict, they may be essential ingredients and some dishes can be rather bland without them; they can be added to taste after the meal is cooked if you wish.

All ingredients are commonly found in large suburban supermarkets. This does not mean that all of the foods will be available all of the time. Don't spend time trying to find a particular ingredient — compromise! For example, choko and zucchini are interchangeable.

Why processed foods?

Human beings have been processing their food for millennia — ever since the discovery of fire in fact. Food was initially processed because of the benefits which resulted. But all types of food processing result in some nutrient loss, irrespective of whether the processing occurs at a domestic or commercial level. However in the extreme, substantial nutrient losses can occur and this can be detrimental to health and well-being. During processing, nutrients are lost because of reactions with other constituents in the food — with oxygen, light or heat or because they are leached out by water.

Reduction in nutrient value of food is usually accompanied by reduction in its sensory qualities of colour, flavour, smell and texture. When you open a packet or can that has been lying about for a while, have a look first, then smell, then prod. If it passes these tests the chances are it's O.K. Foods in good condition usually retain a substantial level of nutrients. If a varied, balanced diet is followed, any one food will make only a small contribution to the total intake of nutrients, and losses resulting from commercial processing will be of little consequence. However, if the diet is restricted, such losses become more significant.

With this proviso in mind, processed, frozen and canned products are extensively used in this book. Dried vegetables however are not used because cooking them removes water soluble nutrients. This book is based on the assumption that the reader is not an expert cook but a typical Australian, handy with the can opener and with a preference for meat and vegetables well done. For this person, the use of canned and frozen foods provides a convenient and nutritious alternative to long, involved preparation and cooking.

Some canned and processed foods may be high in salt and sugar. However, many manufacturers are now reducing the concentration of these ingredients in their product lines. Read labels before you buy. Ingredients lists on labels are in order of weight. If,

for example, a chicken soup label lists its ingredients as sugar, chicken, salt, then there is more sugar in that can than chicken. Choose a brand containing more chicken than sugar. All words ending in '-ose' are sugars, for example, glucose, sucrose, lactose, fructose. However they are not all equal in sweetness; a little fructose has the same intensity of sweetness as a larger quantity of glucose.

Salt is sodium chloride. Other salty tasting chemicals often used in processed food, include sodium nitrite and monosodium glutamate. Excess sodium should be avoided. In the case of many canned products, most of the salt is in the brine. If this is drained off much of the excess salt is removed. Smoked products usually contain sodium nitrite. Cheese can be high in salt so do not have more than one dish containing salt at each meal.

There is no evidence to suggest that a healthy person need remove salt and sugar completely from the diet. Indeed it would be extremely difficult to do so. However, it is a healthy practice to avoid excess.

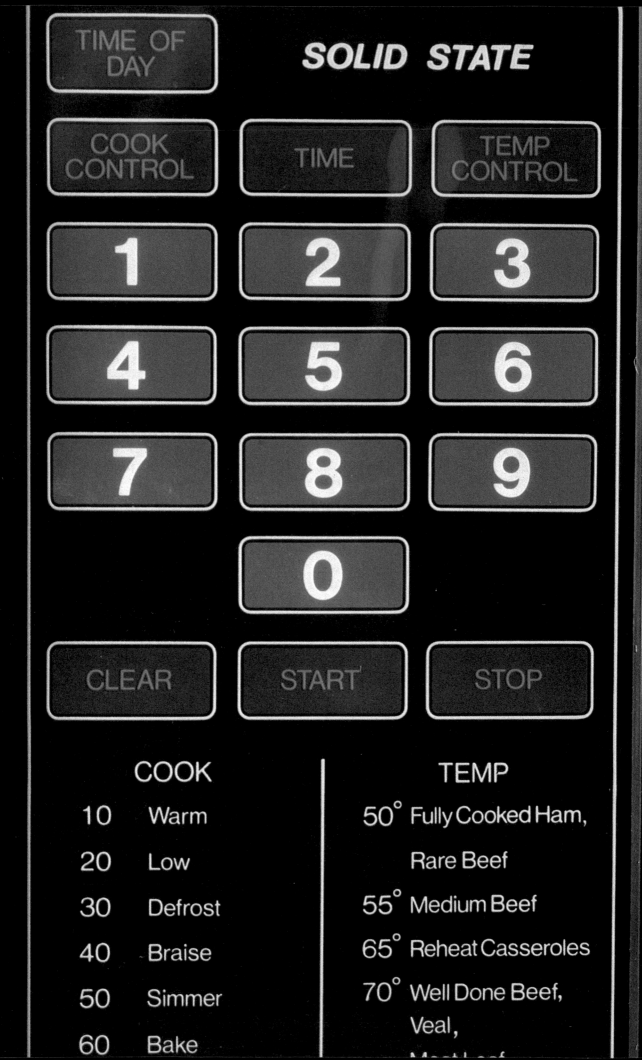

THE MICROWAVE OVEN

What type of oven

Buy the smallest size if space is a problem. Otherwise a larger oven size is more practical. The cost depends on the gadgetry. You don't need one with memory for the recipes in this book. The less buttons and dials the better. What is needed is a lever of some type to open the door, an on–off button and two or three cooking speeds — high, low and maybe defrost.

A turntable is not essential although most brands have them. The cheaper types simply have a removable tray on the bottom. This is adequate provided the fan system is good.

The fan is an essential feature which disperses the waves for even cooking. The house brands of department stores can be just as effective as well known trade names.

What you can cook

Almost anything. Egg and pasta need a little skill and meat doesn't brown. Pop a potato in the oven, cook it two to three minutes, slit, add butter and you have a royal treat! Vegetables are quick and easy to cook in a microwave and everyone needs to eat more vegetables. You can heat a pie in a paper bag and soup in a plate or a paper cup or revamp the Chinese meal you bought on the way home. Leftover percolated coffee, or cold tea from a teapot can be reheated.

Grains and grain products can be a problem because of their low water content. All microwave cookbooks provide cereal recipes, but pasta and rice will take almost as long to cook as by conventional methods. Although many beginners have problems with cooking their winter porridge at first, it is worthwhile persevering as it is really quite simple.

Sauces can be difficult to thicken because the cooking method is so fast. Use prepared sauces or canned soups instead. Jams and puréed fruits are also acceptable. Tomato purée is another alternative. Baby foods such as stewed apple are packaged in amounts ideal for one serve and have a multitude of uses.

Meat is easy to cook if you remember that shape, size and density are important (and keep in mind that it does not brown). Boneless meat will cook more uniformly than meat on the bone. Pile sauce or mushrooms on top of steak or chops when cooking. The flavour will improve and you won't see the colour of the meat!

The flavours of herbs and spices do not diffuse through a dish and mellow as they do in conventional cooking because of the brevity of cooking time and lack of dilution. So take care that you do not add too much. More flavouring can always be added later if needed.

How to cook it

For the absolutely lazy, disposable paper cups and plates can be used. When cooking whole vegetables such as a corn cob or jacket potato, a paper towel on the bottom of the oven is an adequate substitute for a plate.

A flat dinner or bread and butter plate is best for arranging a meal of meat and whole vegetables. If cooking vegetables alone follow recipe directions.

If different types of food are to be cooked together on a plate, cut in similar sized pieces, otherwise smaller pieces will be cooked first. Thicker portions of food should be placed on the outside. Low moisture foods such as root vegetables should also be arranged on the outside of the plate in small pieces whilst high moisture leafy vegetables should be in the centre.

For leftovers, use glass jars with wide openings, dessert plates or glass bowls. Lids should not be used, but cover jar openings with greaseproof paper to avoid splattering and drying out. Don't cook eggs in their shells. They will explode unless treated properly. Adding eggs to leftovers is probably the most successful way of using them. Do not use containers with a narrow neck opening or any metal trim.

Generally, less liquid is required than in conventional cooking, so canned products may need to be drained. Check the recipe carefully before commencing.

VEGETABLES

The microwave oven performs best with vegetables. If cooked properly they retain flavour, colour and nutrients. Use the minimum of water in cooking. Various cooking styles are given but all vegetables can be cooked with only residual water from washing.

Instead of using salt try various herbs for extra flavour. Oregano and dill enhance tomatoes. Sprinkle cumin on zucchini and nutmeg on corn. Experiment. Various combinations of fruits potentiate flavours in vegetables; for example, oranges and carrots are a successful combination.

Try a meatless meal sometime. Simply dress up the vegetables for the main meal and add cheese or eggs for protein.

Asparagus with Sesame Sauce

½ can asparagus cuts, drained
¼ cup unsalted butter
1 teaspoon vinegar
2 teaspoons sesame seeds

Arrange asparagus on a flat serving dish. Melt butter in a cup for 30 seconds. Stir in vinegar and sesame seeds. Pour over asparagus and heat for 2 minutes.

Easy Asparagus with Butter Sauce

1 can asparagus spears
½ cup unsalted butter
1 clove garlic, crushed
juice 1 small lemon
pinch cinnamon

Choose a good brand of asparagus with thin green spears. Remove from can, drain and place on serving dish.

Melt butter in a cup for 30 seconds. Pour melted butter over asparagus. Pour over lemon juice and sprinkle with cinnamon. Cook for 2 minutes.

Fresh Asparagus

1 small bunch fresh asparagus

Wash asparagus and arrange on flat serving dish. Cover with greaseproof paper and cook for 4–6 minutes or until tender (time will depend on thickness of spears). Do not allow colour change to occur.

Artichoke Hearts with Horseradish

1 can or jar artichoke hearts
1 tablespoon unsalted butter
1 teaspoon horseradish

Drain 4 artichoke hearts and place on a small serving dish. Heat through on low for 1 minute.

Combine butter and horseradish in small glass dish or cup and heat, covered, for 1½ minutes, being careful with the hot fat. Mix well.

Pour sauce over artichokes and return for brief reheating — about 50 seconds.

Valentine Salad

½ can hearts of palm
½ can baby beetroot
oil and vinegar dressing

Arrange well drained hearts of palm on a serving plate and heat on low for 1½ minutes.

Halve beetroot and dice 4 of the halves. Set the rest aside. Place in a glass bowl, pour in dressing and cook on low for 1 minute.

Place diced beetroot in centre of hearts on the serving plate and encircle with remaining baby beetroot halves.

Beans with Corn

½ cup frozen beans
½ cup frozen corn pieces or
  canned corn kernels, drained
1 small can diced capsicum,
  drained

Combine all ingredients, place in glass bowl and cover with lid or paper towel. Cook for 5 minutes.

Sautéed Beans

2 tablespoons unsalted butter
1 cup frozen green beans
pinch oregano

Melt butter in glass jar or cup for 30 seconds. Place beans on serving dish and cook for 5 minutes. Add oregano to butter and mix. Toss over beans and serve immediately.

Beans Polish Style

1 cup frozen broad beans
1 onion, chopped
½ cup green olives, chopped
¼ cup mayonnaise
¼ cup grated Parmesan cheese
1 boiled egg

Mix beans, onion and olives. Place in a medium-sized glass bowl and add 1 tablespoon water. Cook for 3 minutes.
  Add mayonnaise and cheese and toss in vegetables. Mix. Cook for 1½ minutes. Chop egg and sprinkle over vegetables just before serving.

Broccoli

1 small bunch fresh broccoli

Separate bunch into florets. Remove thick stalks and break into small segments. Wash well but do not dry. Arrange on serving plate. Cover and cook for 5 minutes.

Broccoli with Tangy Sauce

1 cup frozen broccoli
1 tablespoon unsalted butter
juice one lemon
½ cup grapefruit segments
(fresh or canned)

Place broccoli in medium-sized glass bowl and cook for 4 minutes. Melt butter in a cup for 30 seconds. Stir in lemon juice.

Arrange grapefruit segments over broccoli and cover with sauce. Return to cook for further 1½ minutes.

Cabbage

1 cup shredded cabbage
1 clove
1 teaspoon unsalted butter

Place well washed cabbage in oven bag. Add other ingredients. Secure with elastic band and pierce bag once with a fork to allow escape of steam. Cook for 5 minutes. Toss bag to mix cabbage.

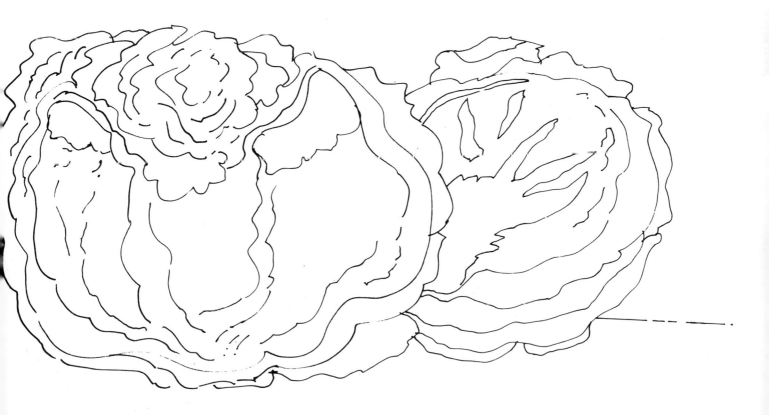

Red Cabbage Supreme

1 cup shredded red cabbage
1 apple, peeled, cored and sliced
1 clove garlic, crushed
1 bay leaf
1 teaspoon brown sugar
1 tablespoon vinegar
½ cup port

Combine all ingredients in a casserole or glass bowl. Cover with lid or greaseproof paper. Cook for 5 minutes.

Serve hot or chilled as an accompaniment to other dishes or as a snack. For added colour and texture serve with pecans, shredded coconut and a sprig of dill.

Potato Allemande

2 potatoes
½ can or jar sauerkraut (pickled cabbage)
¼ cup milk
1 tablespoon cooking oil

Drain sauerkraut. Place potatoes on paper towel and cook for 4 minutes.

Remove potato skins. In a medium-sized glass bowl, mash potatoes with a fork. Add milk and cooking oil. Mix well. Add sauerkraut and stir through. Cook on low for 2½ minutes.

Cauliflower

500 g cauliflower
½ cup water
1 teaspoon dried tarragon

Prepare cauliflower by separating florets, removing thick stalks and breaking into segments. Bring water to the boil with tarragon in covered casserole dish or glass bowl. Add cauliflower, cover and cook for 6–8 minutes.

Cream of Cauliflower Soup

⅓ cup frozen cauliflower
½ teaspoon mustard
½ can Vichyssoise soup
¼ cup sherry
½ cup hot water
1 tablespoon sour cream
1 tablespoon chopped parsley or chives

Cook frozen cauliflower in large glass bowl for 2 minutes. Combine mustard, Vichyssoise, sherry and water. Add to cauliflower. Cook for 2 minutes.

Remove and stir in sour cream and parsley. Cover and let stand for 5 minutes.

Red Cabbage Supreme

Cauliflower Sorrel

500 g cauliflower
small bunch sorrel or spinach or
  few outer lettuce leaves
2 tablespoons unsalted butter
½ cup flaked almonds

Wash cauliflower and remove thick stalks. Break up cauliflower and place florets in glass bowl. Add 1 tablespoon butter. Wash sorrel leaves and remove tough stems. Shred finely.

Cover cauliflower with shredded leaves and sprinkle with flaked almonds. Add remaining butter. Cover with lid or paper towel and cook for 6–8 minutes.

Carrots

2 medium-sized carrots

Top and tail carrots. Wash well and cut into quarters. Place on a serving plate. Cook for 4 minutes.

Herbed Carrots

1 cup diced or sliced frozen carrot
½ cup canned Cream of Celery
  soup
½ cup canned Cream of
  Mushroom soup
pinch dried thyme
pinch dried marjoram or oregano
few button mushrooms (optional)
½ cup breadcrumbs
1 teaspoon unsalted butter
1 tablespoon chopped fresh
  parsley or basil
Parmesan cheese (optional)

Mix first 5 ingredients and button mushrooms if used and place in a glass bowl or casserole dish. Melt butter in a cup for 30 seconds. Toss breadcrumbs into butter, stir and sprinkle over mixture.

Cook for 6 minutes. Serve garnished with fresh parsley or basil and Parmesan cheese if liked.

Step 1: Combine carrot, soups and herbs in a glass bowl

Step 2: Toss breadcrumbs in melted butter, sprinkle over mixture and cook for 6 minutes

Step 3: Garnish with fresh parsley or basil and Parmesan cheese

Hot Carrot and Leek Salad

1 large carrot
1 leek
10 mL cooking oil
10 mL vinegar
½ teaspoon mustard
2 tablespoons currants
few snow peas (optional)

Slice carrot very thinly. Use only white stem of the leek and discard green part. Wash well and slice thinly. Shake oil, vinegar and mustard together in a screw top jar.

Mix together carrot, leek, currants and snow peas if used and add oil and vinegar mixture. Toss all together. Arrange in a glass bowl or casserole dish, cover with lid or greaseproof paper and cook for 5 minutes.

This hot salad may be eaten on its own or served as an accompaniment.

Cointreau Carrots

1 medium-sized carrot, thickly
    sliced
1 tablespoon grated orange rind
    or candied citrus peel
1 liqueur glass Cointreau
1 tablespoon honey

Place sliced carrot and Cointreau in a small glass mixing bowl or ramekin. Sprinkle orange rind over carrot and pour over honey.

Cover with lid or greaseproof paper and cook for 4–6 minutes. Allow to stand for 2 minutes after removing from oven.

Ginger Carrots

½ cup frozen diced carrots
2 tablespoons unsalted butter
¼ cup crystallized ginger
¼ teaspoon ground ginger
1 tablespoon orange juice

Place all ingredients in oven bag. Secure with elastic band and pierce once with a fork to release steam. Cook for 3 minutes.

Carrot with Sultanas

1 carrot, grated
½ cup sultanas
¼ cup claret

Mix all ingredients and place in a ramekin. Cook for 3 minutes.

Hot Carrot and Leek Salad

Ratatouille

1 eggplant (unpeeled)
1 medium–sized choko or
* zucchini*
1 can peeled tomatoes
1 onion, chopped
1 small capsicum, chopped
chives or parsley

If using choko, cut in half and peel under running water. Remove seed. Remove green stem of eggplant. Cut in half then dice into pieces about 3 cm across. Dice choko or zucchini into same size pieces. Add all other ingredients and mix well.

Place in large glass mixing bowl or casserole. Cover with lid or greaseproof paper and cook on low heat for 10 minutes. Garnish with finely chopped chives or parsley and serve with fresh, crusty bread and a salad.

This amount is ample for at least 2 meals. Refrigerate unused portion — it will keep for at least 48 hours.

When required for reheating, add 1 teaspoon water and reheat for approximately 1 minute, depending on quantity. Stir and reheat for further minute.

Step 1: Dice choko, eggplant and zucchini into 3 cm pieces

Step 2: Add remaining ingredients and mix well

Baked Eggplant

1 small eggplant, peeled and
* sliced*
1 small onion, chopped

Place all ingredients in oven bag. Seal with elastic band. Pierce once with a fork to release steam. Cook for 5 minutes.

Minted Peas

1 cup frozen peas
1 tablespoon crème de menthe

Place all ingredients in small ramekin. Cover with lid or greaseproof paper and cook for 2 minutes.

Peas and Cucumber

⅓ cucumber, peeled and diced
1 cup frozen peas
¼ cup cream
½ teaspoon vinegar
pinch nutmeg

Place peas and cucumber in glass mixing bowl. Cover and cook for 2 minutes. Add vinegar and nutmeg and mix well. Cook for 30 seconds. Stir in cream.

Pea Stuffed Pears

2 canned pear halves
   (unsweetened)
½ cup frozen peas
mint leaves

Arrange pear halves on serving plate. Place a mint leaf in each hollow and top with peas. Cook for 4 minutes.

Country Style Peas

1 cup frozen peas
1 outside lettuce leaf
2 shallots, chopped
1 teaspoon unsalted butter

Shred lettuce and mix well with other ingredients. Place in glass bowl, cover with lid or greaseproof paper and cook for 2 minutes.

Stuffed Potato

1 large potato
¼ cup ricotta cheese
1 teaspoon sesame seeds
sesame seeds and 1 or 2 button
   mushrooms for garnish

Wash and dry potato. Pierce with fork in 2 or 3 places. Place potato on paper towel and cook for 4–6 minutes, turning half way through cooking time.

   Remove potato from oven and split with a sharp knife. Mix sesame seeds and ricotta cheese together and place in split. Garnish with toasted sesame seeds and sliced button mushrooms. Variation: Add a little finely diced ham and some cracked black pepper to ricotta mixture before filling potato.

Stuffed Potato

Baked Potato

1 medium-sized potato,
    (unpeeled)
unsalted butter

Wash and dry potato. Pierce with fork in 2 or 3 places depending on size. Arrange on paper towel and cook for 4-6 minutes, turning half way through cooking time.

Remove and split with a sharp knife. Place butter in split.

Mashed Potatoes

3 potatoes (unpeeled)
¼ cup cream
1 tablespoon chopped parsley

Wash and dry potatoes. Pierce with a fork in 2 or 3 places. Arrange on paper towel and cook for 10-12 minutes. Remove skins. Place in glass bowl, mash and add other ingredients. Pat down with fork. Cook for 2 more minutes.

Sweet Potato Parmesan

1 medium-sized sweet potato
1 medium-sized parsnip
1 bacon rasher, chopped
½ cup grated Parmesan cheese
2 tablespoons water
1 small onion, chopped

Wash, peel and cut sweet potato and parsnip into rounds. Place in large glass bowl or casserole and add bacon, onion and water. Cover with lid or paper towel and cook for 6 minutes.

Top with Parmesan cheese. Cook for 2 minutes or until cheese begins to melt. Garnish with snipped chives.

Served with extra Parmesan cheese and a glass of white wine this dish is a meal in itself.

Variation: For extra colour and flavour add some diced capsicum to the mixture before cooking.

Step 1: Wash and peel sweet potato and parsnip and cut into rounds

Step 2: Place vegetables in bowl and add chopped bacon and onion

Step 3: Top with Parmesan cheese and cook for 2 minutes

Sweet Potato

1 medium–sized sweet potato,
  (unpeeled)

Wash sweet potato and pierce skin with fork. Place on paper towel and cook whole for 15 minutes.

Sweet Potato Bake

1 large sweet potato
2 rounds fresh pineapple, peeled
  and cored
1 tablespoon brown sugar
2 tablespoons unsalted butter
pinch nutmeg

Peel sweet potato and cut into thin rounds. Arrange on a serving dish. Cover with pineapple.

Melt butter in small glass jar for 30 seconds. Add sugar and nutmeg. Shake and let stand for 1 minute until sugar has dissolved. Pour over pineapple and potato mixture. Cook for 7 minutes.

Pumpkin

350–400 g pumpkin

Cut pumpkin into 4 or 5 pieces. Remove seeds but retain skin. Place on paper towel and cook for 6–7 minutes.

Sweet Pumpkin Annie

400 g pumpkin, seeded and peeled
½ can pineapple pieces
1 tablespoon honey

Slice pumpkin into pieces about the size of thick potato chips. Arrange pumpkin and pineapple pieces alternately on a serving dish. Mix honey with pineapple juice and spoon carefully over the pieces. Cook for 4½ minutes.

Leftovers with Tomato

½ cup chopped, cooked leftover
  meat
½ cup chopped, cooked leftover
  vegetables
1 cup diced tomato
1 egg
½ cup grated Parmesan cheese

Combine meat, vegetables and tomato in glass bowl. Beat egg and pour over mixture. Cook for 3 minutes.

Top with grated cheese and cook for 2 minutes or until cheese has melted. Serve with rice for a hearty and nourishing meal.

Herbed Tomato

1 large ripe tomato
pinch oregano
1 teaspoon dried dill

Wash tomato and cut in half. Sprinkle halves with oregano and dill. Arrange on paper towel and cook for 1½ minutes.

Winter Tomato Savoury

1 tomato
1 teaspoon Stilton or blue vein cheese
1 teaspoon chopped chives or parsley

Cut tomato in half and place on flat serving plate. Cook for 1 minute.

Crumble cheese on top of tomato halves and cook on low for 1 minute. Sprinkle with chopped chives before serving.

Willy Nilly

¼ cup diced broccoli stalks
¼ cup diced cauliflower stalks
1 onion, chopped
1 potato, peeled and diced
¼ cup (at least) diced, leftover meat
1 packet French Onion soup
dash angostura bitters
1 cup water

Add water to French Onion soup powder. Mix well to eliminate lumps. Add angostura bitters and mix. Add other ingredients.

Place in small glass bowl and cover with lid or greaseproof paper. Cook for 5 minutes.

Zucchini

2 zucchini (unpeeled)

Wash zucchini and prick in several places with fork. Place on a paper towel and cook for 2 minutes.

Zucchini au Gratin

2 medium-sized zucchini (unpeeled)
2 tablespoons unsalted butter
½ cup breadcrumbs

Cut zucchini into about 3 cm lengths and place in glass bowl. Melt butter in cup for 30 seconds and pour over zucchini. Roll zucchini in butter so they are well coated.

Cover with breadcrumbs. Cover with greaseproof paper and cook for 2 minutes.

Zucchini au Gratin

Zucchini with Cheese

2 small zucchini (unpeeled)
1 tablespoon grated cheese
pinch coriander
Parmesan cheese
cracked black pepper

Cut zucchini lengthwise. Sprinkle with coriander, grated cheese and Parmesan cheese and pepper. Place on serving dish, cover and cook for 2 minutes.

Cider Parsnip

1 parsnip
1 teaspoon honey
2 tablespoons cider

Scrape parsnip and cut into quarters lengthwise. Place in shallow casserole dish.

Add honey to cider and pour over parsnips. Cook for 2 minutes then let stand for at least 1 minute.

Choko

1 choko

Skin choko under water. Cut in half and remove seed. Add 1 teaspoon water to seed hollow. Cook for 4 minutes.

Choko with Onion

1 choko
1 onion

Skin choko under water. Remove seed and cut into eighths. Skin the onion and cut into small pieces.

Place onion in oven bag with choko and secure with rubber band. Pierce to let out steam. Cook for 4 minutes.

Gumbo

300 g okra
1 onion
1 tablespoon water

Remove stems from okra and chop finely in rounds. Do not attempt to remove seeds. Chop onion into similar sized pieces.

Combine all ingredients in casserole dish and cook for 4 minutes. Stir. Cook another minute if necessary. The consistency should be soft and sticky.

FRUIT

Fruit is Nature's sweet convenience food. It is high in Vitamin C, some B group vitamins and carotene. Vitamin C is destroyed by heat. Treat fruits tenderly as bruising also destroys nutrients.

At the end of this section are also included several recipes for warm and fortifying drink concoctions.

Crème de Menthe Pears

Creme de Menthe Pears

2 canned pear halves
2 teaspoons lemon juice
2 tablespoons crème de menthe
1 serve ice cream
shreds of orange peel, blanched

Drain pear halves, reserving syrup. Pour syrup into large glass jar. Add lemon juice and crème de menthe and heat for 1 minute.

Add pears to liquid in jar. Put on lid and invert so that liquid pours over fruit. Serve either hot or cold with ice cream. Rum and a pinch of nutmeg can be substituted for the crème de menthe. Garnish with orange peel shreds.

Remaining pears in can can be stored for 2–3 days in refrigerator and served as an accompaniment to lamb or pork.

Whole, peeled, fresh pears may be substituted for canned pear halves when entertaining.

34

Hot Apple Slice

1 bought apple slice
1 tablespoon honey
cinnamon

Brush honey over top of apple slice and sprinkle cinnamon over sparingly. Heat for 1 minute. Check that slice is heated through completely.

Champagne Peaches

2 canned peach halves
1 cup champagne or white grape
   juice
1 clove

Place all ingredients in a glass jar. Liquid should cover the peaches, if not, add extra liquid. Cook for 2½ minutes. Cover with lid and refrigerate when cool. Will keep at least 48 hours.

Gingered Banana Ice Cream

1 serve ice cream
½ cup chopped unsalted walnuts
   or macadamia nuts
3 tablespoons honey
3 tablespoons water
1 teaspoon unsalted butter
1 tablespoon chopped ginger in
   syrup
1 banana, sliced

Place ice cream in a dessert plate and sprinkle with nuts. Put in freezer. Combine honey, water, butter, ginger and banana in a glass jar and cook for 2 minutes until mushy. Cool. Pour over ice cream and eat immediately.

Mango Sauce

2 ripe mangoes
2 tablespoons apricot nectar
1 teaspoon chopped ginger root
   (optional)
1 chilli, finely chopped
1 teaspoon sesame seeds

Peel mangoes and remove seed. Cut into small pieces and place in a glass jar with apricot nectar. Add ginger, chilli and sesame seeds and mix well.

   Cook for 2 minutes. Mix and test consistency. If necessary cook another minute or two.

Oriental Sauce

½ cup canned lychees
1 teaspoon curry powder
1 small glass port
1 tablespoon apricot nectar
½ cup cream

Blend first four ingredients in blender or food processor. Cook in a glass jar for 3 minutes.

   Mix in cream when cool to produce a smooth, velvety sauce.

Stewed Apple

2 large green apples
1 tablespoon sugar
½ cup water
½ teaspoon nutmeg

Peel apple and cut into small pieces. Place in large glass bowl and mix in sugar. Add water.

   Cook for 4 minutes until apple is soft and moisture absorbed. When soft, sprinkle nutmeg on top and let stand.

   The apple can get very hot so allow to cool a little before eating.

Pears in Wine

2 whole pears
1 cup white wine
pinch cinnamon

Wash pears. Prick skin in a few places with a fork and place in small glass bowl. Add wine and cinnamon.

   Cook on low for 5 minutes. Turn pears over and cook for 2 minutes on full.

Tamarillos

2 tamarillos (tree tomatoes)
pinch cumin

Cut tamarillos in half and arrange cut side up on a flat serving plate. Sprinkle with cumin. Cook for 2½ minutes.

Remove pulp from tough outer skin with a teaspoon. Serve with meat or ice cream.

Pickled Plums

2 cups very ripe plums
1 cup brown sugar
1 cup white wine vinegar
pinch cinnamon

Boil sugar, vinegar and cinnamon for 2 minutes in a large glass jar. Add washed, pricked plums and cook for 2 minutes. Check that plums do not start disintegrating.

Cook for 1–2 minutes longer. Cool. Screw lid on jar and store in refrigerator.

Hot Pineapple Rings

2 canned pineapple rings
½ cup pineapple juice
small pinch powdered ginger

Place rings side by side on a serving plate. Stir ginger into juice in can. Mix well. Pour juice over rings and cook for 2 minutes.

Baked Pawpaw

1 small firm pawpaw, yellow but
   not quite ready for eating
2 tablespoons Cointreau
¼ cup chopped unsalted nuts
1 tablespoon honey

Split pawpaw in half and scoop out seeds. Do not peel. Spoon 1 tablespoon Cointreau into each cavity. Combine nuts with honey and pour into cavity.

Place on paper towel and cook for 3 minutes. Let stand for 2 minutes before serving.

Spirited Nightcap

1 orange and cinnamon teabag
1 liqueur glass Grand Marnier or
   Chartreuse
1 slice orange

Make 1 cup orange and cinnamon tea. Add liqueur and orange. Stir and reheat for 1 minute.

Cherries in Kirsch

½ can pitted cherries
½ liqueur glass Kirsch
pinch cinnamon

Place cherries in glass jar and cover with juice. Cook until mixture just begins to boil then add cinnamon and Kirsch.
   Screw lid on tightly and leave for ½ hour until cherries are cool and flavours have diffused.

Mulled Wine

½ cup claret
½ cup port
1 tablespoon currants
¼ teaspoon cinnamon or 1
   cinnamon stick

Combine all ingredients in a measuring jug and heat for 2 minutes. Serve in a tall glass with a strawberry and a lemon twist.

Venus Potion

1 rosehip teabag
1 liqueur glass Marsala
1 clove

Make 1 cup rosehip tea and pour into measuring jug. Add Marsala and clove.
   Heat on low for 2½ minutes. Let stand for 5 minutes before removing clove. Reheat if required.

Mulled Wine

CEREALS

Unrefined cereals are high in fibre and some of the B group vitamins. Remember that cereals swell when they take in fluid. Roughly ¼ cup uncooked cereal makes up 1 cup when cooked. Overcatering is not a problem since cooked cereals keep well in the refrigerator. When reheating, care should be taken against drying out.

Sweet Corn

1 small frozen corn cob

Place cob on paper towel and cook for 2 minutes.

Baby Corn Cobs

1 small can baby corn cobs

Transfer contents of can to small glass bowl, cover with greaseproof paper and cook for 3–4 minutes.

Spaghetti, Macaroni or Noodles

*1 cup spaghetti, macaroni or
    noodles*
3 cups water
1 tablespoon cooking oil

Bring water to the boil in a large glass bowl or 4-cup measuring jug. Carefully pour in oil over the back of a spoon so that film is formed on top of water. This stops the pasta sticking together.

Add pasta, making sure it is coated with oil. Cook, covered, for 15 minutes or until soft. Drain.

Spaghetti with Ricotta

¼ packet spaghetti
1 clove garlic, crushed
⅓ cup milk
125 mL cream
200 g ricotta cheese
½ cup grated Parmesan cheese

Boil 4 cups water in a large glass bowl. Add spaghetti, making sure it is covered with water. Cook, covered, for 15 minutes.

While spaghetti is cooking, combine garlic, milk and cream. When spaghetti is cooked, drain in a colander. Meanwhile heat milk mixture for 30 seconds in a measuring jug. Add cheeses and whisk until smooth. Cook for 1 minute. Stir.

Mix sauce with drained spaghetti. Add more Parmesan cheese to taste.

Polenta

½ cup yellow cornmeal or polenta
2 cups water
½ cup grated Parmesan cheese
pinch cayenne pepper

Measure cornmeal into a large glass mixing bowl. Add water and stir well. Cook for 4 minutes. Add cheese and pepper and cook for 1½ minutes.

Let stand, covered, for 5 minutes. Wrap in greaseproof paper, refrigerate and cut into slices when required. To reheat, place slice on paper towel and heat for 50 seconds.

Serve as an accompaniment or as a meal in itself with red cabbage and snow peas, garnished with button mushrooms.

Egg Noodles and Broccoli

1 cup broccoli florets
½ cup chopped shallots
½ cup pine nuts
1 cup cooked egg noodles or
    spaghetti

Place broccoli, shallots and pine nuts in an oven bag; secure with rubber band. Pierce bag with fork to allow steam to escape.

Cook for 2½ minutes. Add noodles and toss. Cook 1 minute more.

Wholemeal Spaghetti with Eggs and Tomato

250 g wholemeal spaghetti
¼ cup chopped parsley
½ cup grated cheese
1 tomato, cut into wedges
1 egg

Cook wholemeal spaghetti, covered, in hot water in a glass mixing bowl until soft. Drain off water. Add parsley and cheese and mix well.

Make a well in the middle of the spaghetti and line with tomato wedges. Break egg into well. Cook for 2½ minutes or until egg is cooked.

Polenta

Wholemeal Semolina Porridge

2 tablespoons wholemeal
    semolina
½ cup milk
glacé fruit (optional)
few pecan and pistachio nuts
    (optional)

Pour milk into a 2–cup measuring jug. Add semolina. Cook, covered for 2 minutes. Stir. Cook for 1 minute. Let stand before serving.

Serve sprinkled with brown sugar, glacé fruit pieces and pecan and pistachio nuts if liked.

First Break Wheat Porridge

3 tablespoons first break wheat
½ cup milk

Soak cereal in water overnight. Drain, discard water and place wheat in large glass bowl. Stir in milk.

Cook for 2 minutes. Stir. Cook a further 2 minutes. Stir. Cover and let stand for 4 minutes before serving.

Oatmeal Porridge

2 tablespoons oatmeal
½ cup milk

Place oatmeal in 2–cup measuring jug and add milk. Stir and let stand for 5 minutes. Cook on low for 3 minutes. Stir. Cook on high 1½ minutes longer. Stir. Cover and let stand a few minutes.

Rice with Currants and Pecans

¼ cup Sun Gold Vita Rice,
    pre–soaked
¼ cup currants or sultanas
½ cup pecan nuts
¼ cup chopped chives

Combine all ingredients and mix well in a glass bowl. Cook for 2 minutes.

NB: Sun Gold Vita Rice can be replaced with other commercially available pre-cooked rice products.

Wholemeal Semolina Porridge

Spinach Fettucine with Sardines

200 g fettucine
1 small can sardines or anchovies
1 tablespoon grated Parmesan
  cheese
¼ red capsicum

Place fettucine in glass mixing bowl and cover with hot water. Cook for 10 minutes. Drain off water.
  Empty can of sardines, including oil, into bowl. Mix well and heat for 30 seconds.
  Garnish with capsicum, sliced into thin strips and Parmesan cheese.

Step 1: Cover fettucine with hot water, cook for 10 minutes then drain off water

Step 2: Mix sardines through fettucine and heat for 30 seconds

Barley with Cauliflower

½ cup pearl barley
1 cup finely chopped cauliflower
  florets
1 tablespoon chopped chives

Cook barley, covered with hot water, in a deep measuring jug for 20 minutes or until grain is soft and swollen.
  Pour off liquid and heat for 30 seconds to evaporate excess liquid. Add cauliflower and chives, mix well and cook for 1 minute more. Cauliflower should still be crunchy.

Sun Gold Vita Rice or Commercially Pre-Cooked Rice

½ cup commercially pre-cooked
  rice
¾ cup hot water

Combine rice and hot water in a large glass bowl and soak for at least 1 hour until all liquid has been absorbed. Cook, covered, for 2 minutes. Let stand for 10 minutes before serving.

NB: Sun Gold Vita Rice can be replaced with other commercially available pre-cooked rice products.

Fettucine with Sardines

Rice with Leftovers

Rice with Leftovers

1 cup cooked rice
½ can asparagus cuts, drained
1 cup cooked white meat pieces
1 small can whole mushrooms in
*   butter sauce*
1 can diced capsicum, drained
2 tablespoons fresh chopped basil
*   (optional)*

Combine all ingredients in a mixing bowl and heat for 1½ minutes. Mix and cook for 1 minute more.
    Serve with vegetables for a hearty meal.

Fried Rice

Step 1: In a large glass bowl combine onion, mushrooms, prawns and almonds, cover and cook 2½ minutes
Step 2: Mix beaten egg into rice, stir in prawn mixture and cook, covered for 3 minutes

Fried Rice

½ cup Sun Gold Vita Rice,
 pre-soaked
1 onion, chopped
1 small can mushrooms in butter
 sauce
1 small can prawns
¼ cup chopped almonds or
 toasted slivered almonds
1 egg
sliced shallots (optional)

Combine onion, mushrooms, prawns and almonds in a large glass bowl. Cover and cook 2½ minutes. Mix beaten egg into rice and stir in prawn mixture. Cook, covered, for 3 minutes. Let stand before serving. Garnish with shallots.

Spiced Rice

1 cup pre-soaked Sun Gold Vita
 Rice
2 saffron threads
¼ teaspoon turmeric
2 cardamon seeds, grated
¼ teaspoon cumin

Mix all ingredients in a bowl, cover with greaseproof paper and cook for 2 minutes.

Wrap dish in a tea towel for at least 10 minutes to retain heat. This allows for diffusion of flavour. If required, reheat for 30 seconds.

Spicy Pumpkin Rice

1 cup cooked, mashed pumpkin
½ cup pre-soaked Sun Gold Vita
 Rice
1 egg
¼ teaspoon powdered ginger
¼ teaspoon cinnamon

Combine pumpkin and rice in mixing bowl. Add egg and stir well. Sprinkle ginger and cinnamon on top. Cook for 2½ minutes.

Spaghetti Dessert

1 egg
½ cup cold milk
1 cup cooked spaghetti
1 tablespoon apricot jam
½ cup sultanas

Beat egg and milk. Combine spaghetti, jam and sultanas and custard mixture in a casserole dish. Cook for 2 minutes.

Beef and Vegetable Kebabs

MEAT, FISH AND CHICKEN

Meat does not brown in microwave ovens to the same extent as in conventional cookers. Use sauces, fruits and vegetables to mask meat and complement flavour.

If meat is overcooked it will be tough and leathery. Because of its widely varying fat content, cooking times given are only approximate. It is better to undercook, check, then cook a little more if necessary than to risk overcooking.

Note: There is some doubt as to whether microwave cooking will kill parasites to the same degree as conventional cooking. So if you've been given a gift of wild game, cook it well!

Abalone with Oyster Sauce

1 can abalone
1 can Cream of Oyster soup
pinch powdered ginger
1 tablespoon white wine

Dilute soup with ½ can water. Add ginger and wine and mix well. Place abalone in medium–sized glass bowl and cover with sauce. Cook on low for 5 minutes.

Lobster Soup

1 can Lobster Bisque
100 g shelled, cooked prawns,
   frozen or fresh
1 teaspoon cream
½ wine glass sherry
sprig of dill for garnish
1 teaspoon sour cream for garnish

Mix soup and prawns in a glass jar. Cook for 2 minutes. Just before serving stir in cream and sherry. Serve with croûtons and garnish with dill and sour cream

Curried Prawns

250 g shelled, cooked prawns,
   frozen or fresh
½ can Cream of Chicken soup
1 teaspoon curry powder
1 tablespoon canned or chopped
   fresh apple

Combine chicken soup and curry powder in a large glass jar and heat for 2 minutes. Stir in prawns and apple. Cover with greaseproof paper and heat for 3 minutes.

Lobster Soup

Lemon Fish

1 frozen fish fillet
1 small onion, chopped
2 slices lemon

Place fish on serving plate. Sprinkle over onion and top with lemon slices. Cook on paper for 2 minutes. Check. Depending on size, a minute more cooking time may be required.

Mackerel with Mushroom Sauce

1 can Cream of Mushroom soup
1 cup milk
½ teaspoon cumin
1 can mackerel
½ cup Weet–bix, Vita–brits, or
    Weeties crumbs

Mix soup with milk and cumin until smooth. Place mackerel in medium-sized glass bowl or casserole dish. Pour soup mixture over fish. Sprinkle crumbs on top to cover. Cook for 3 minutes.

Prawns with Vegetables

200 g shelled, cooked prawns,
    fresh or frozen
½ cup chopped onion
2 cauliflower florets
2 broccoli florets
1 medium–sized carrot, thinly
    sliced
¼ cup coarsely chopped capsicum
½ can peeled tomatoes
½ can Onion soup
1 tablespoon sherry

Combine prawns, onion, cauliflower, broccoli, carrot and capsicum. Place in a large glass bowl, cover with greaseproof paper and cook for 3 minutes.

Meanwhile mix tomato, soup and sherry together and stir mixture into vegetables. Cook for 3 minutes more. Let stand for 2 minutes before serving.

This amount is enough for 2 meals. Refrigerate half. Before next serving, add 1 tablespoon water and reheat for 2 minutes.

Step 1: Place prawns, onion, cauliflower, broccoli, carrot and capsicums in bowl, cover and cook for 3 minutes

Step 2: Mix together tomatoes, soup and sherry

Step 3: Stir into vegetable mixture and cook a further 3 minutes

T-Bone with Red Wine Sauce

1 T-bone steak
½ can Cream of Celery soup
1 onion, chopped
¼ cup red wine
2 tomatoes, chopped or 1 can
  peeled tomatoes
1 zucchini, sliced lengthwise

Blend soup with red wine. Add tomato and onion. Place in medium-sized bowl or casserole and cover. Cook on low for 4 minutes. Remove and let stand.

Place steak on serving plate and arrange zucchini beside it. Cook for 2 minutes. To serve, pour red wine sauce over steak.

Western Style Beef

350 g minced beef
1 can baked beans
½ onion, chopped
1 tablespoon horseradish
½ teaspoon ginger

Mix all ingredients and place in a glass bowl or casserole dish. Cook for 3 minutes, stir and cook for further 2 minutes.

Sausages with Prunes and Apple

2 pork sausages
½ cup pitted prunes
1 jar cooked apple baby food
¼ teaspoon thyme

Cut each sausage into 4 pieces and prick skin. Place in glass bowl and cook for 2 minutes.

Combine all other ingredients and add to sausage. Mix. Cook for 2 minutes then let stand for at least 1 minute.

Beef and Vegetable Kebabs

1 tablespoon teriyaki sauce
1 tablespoon honey
½ clove garlic, crushed
1 tablespoon dry sherry
⅛ teaspoon ground ginger
1 beef steak, thick cut
6 cherry tomatoes
4 spring onions
½ capsicum
6 button mushrooms

Combine first 5 ingredients in a bowl. Cut steak into cubes and add to the mixture. Marinate for 1 hour.

Wash and dry tomatoes. Trim spring onions and cut capsicum into squares. Wash and trim mushrooms.

Thread beef and vegetables alternately on skewers. Cook on medium for 1½ minutes. Brush kebabs with marinade and heat a further 20 seconds on high.

Serve with a crisp salad or fried rice.

Fillet Steak with Mushrooms

1 fillet steak
1 can mushrooms in butter sauce

Place steak on serving dish. Pour mushrooms over meat and cook for 2 minutes.

Beef with Mango Sauce

2 slices roast beef
1 teaspoon horseradish
Mango sauce (see recipe under
   FRUIT)

Thinly spread beef with horseradish, cover with mango sauce and cook for 2 minutes.

Fillet Steak with Piquant Sauce

1 piece eye fillet
3–4 anchovy or sardine fillets
1 egg
1 teaspoon brandy
2 teaspoons Dijon mustard
½ onion, chopped
1 tablespoon chopped dill pickles
1 slice fresh or canned pineapple

Cook steak on serving dish for 2 minutes. Meanwhile make sauce by mashing sardines or anchovies in bowl with egg, brandy and mustard. Mix well. Add onion and pickles.

When meat is ready, remove from oven and cover completely with sauce. Return meat to oven and cook on low for 1½ minutes. Let stand for 1 minute before serving.

Serve with pineapple rings. Snow peas, mushrooms and cherry tomatoes make ideal accompaniments.

Tamarillo T-Bone

1 T–bone steak
1 tamarillo

Cut tamarillo in half and arrange beside T-bone on serving dish. Cook for 2 minutes or less if steak is preferred rare.

Scoop tamarillo pulp out of skin with teaspoon and pile on top of steak. Reheat for 1 minute.

T-Bone Special

1 T–bone steak
½ can Celery soup
1 can mushrooms in butter
1 tablespoon Tomato Magic

Arrange T-bone on serving plate and cook on low for 2 minutes. Cover with sauce to serve.

Stir together mushrooms and celery soup. Add Tomato Magic and dilute with about ¼ cup water if required. Mix well.

Cook for 2 minutes on high for medium steak, longer for well done.

Cabbage with Mince

1 cup minced meat
¼ cabbage
1 can peeled tomatoes
1 tablespoon tomato pusle

Cook mince for 3 minutes. Shred cabbage. Combine with tomato and paste in bowl and mix well. Cover cabbage mixture with mince and cook for 4 minutes.

Fillet Steak with Piquant Sauce

Beef in Red Wine

1 cup cooked beef, cut into thin
    strips
½ cup red wine
2 whole peppercorns
3 tablespoons vinegar
½ cup sultanas
½ cup walnuts
chopped shallots for garnish

In a medium–sized glass bowl mix wine and vinegar and add peppercorns and sultanas. Marinate beef in the mixture for 15 minutes. Stir in walnuts. Cook for 2 minutes, stir and cook for further 2 minutes. Garnish with shallots and serve with any short pasta.

Step 1: Mix wine and vinegar in a medium-sized bowl and add peppercorns and sultanas

Step 2: Marinate beef in mixture for 15 minutes

Step 3: Stir in walnuts and cook 4 minutes stirring once during cooking

Chicken Curry

¼ teaspoon turmeric
¼ teaspoon powdered ginger
¼ teaspoon cayenne pepper
2 tablespoons cold pressed
    sunflower oil
1 chicken breast

Combine spices with oil in a cup and heat for 50 seconds. Let stand. Arrange chicken on dinner plate. Pour over curry mixture and cook for 2 minutes. Serve with Sun Gold Vita Rice.

Chicken Medley

1 cup chopped cooked chicken or 1
    whole chicken breast, chopped
1 can Cream of Chicken soup
1 tomato, chopped
¼ cup sliced, stuffed olives
1 jar stewed apple baby food
1 clove garlic, crushed
1 tablespoon sherry

Combine all ingredients and mix well. Place in a large glass bowl. Cover with greaseproof paper and cook for 3 minutes.

Mustard Chicken

1 cooked chicken piece
1 tablespoon mustard powder

Rub chicken over with mustard powder. Cook on serving dish for 1½ minutes.

Chicken Tropicana

1 cup chopped cooked chicken
1 banana, peeled
1 can mango or 1 fresh mango,
  peeled and sliced
1 can tomatoes
½ cup ginger wine or white wine
1 clove garlic, crushed
1 small choko, peeled and cored

Chop banana and choko into bite size chunks. Combine with chicken, mango, tomato and garlic and mix well.

Place mixture into a large glass bowl. Cover with paper towel and cook on low for 4 minutes.

Allow to stand for 3 minutes before eating to allow diffusion of flavour. Zucchini may be used instead of choko.

Pork Chop with Onions and Lychees

1 pork chop
1 tablespoon dry sherry
1 teaspoon Cointreau
  1 tablespoon honey
1 onion, thinly sliced
½ can lychees, drained

Blend Cointreau and honey together to make a thick paste. Add onion. Arrange chop on a serving plate and surround with lychees.

Cover chop and lychees with onion mixture. Cook for 3 minutes or until well done.

Chicken Tropicana

Pork and Bitters

1 pork chop or piece pork fillet
Dijon mustard
1 potato, peeled and sliced
2 medium-sized onions, sliced
¼ cup diced celery
½ can tomato purée
1 teaspoon angostura bitters
1 jar stewed apple baby food
cherry tomatoes for garnish

Rub pork with mustard. Let stand. Arrange vegetables in layers in a glass bowl or casserole. Add tomato purée, and angostura bitters.

Cook on low for 10 minutes. Remove vegetables from oven, cover and let stand. Cook meat on serving dish for 2½ minutes. Pork must be well cooked.

Arrange vegetables around pork and pour over apple. Heat for 1 minute. Garnish with cherry tomatoes.

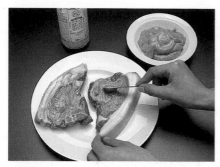

Step 1: Spread mustard over pork and let stand

Step 2: In a glass bowl or casserole arrange vegetables in layers

Step 3: Add tomato purée and angostura bitters to vegetables and cook on low for 10 minutes

Pork with Plum Sauce

1 pork chop
1 tablespoon plum jam
pinch cinnamon

Mix cinnamon with plum jam. Make several small cuts on surface of chops and arrange on a serving dish. Cover and cook for 2 minutes.

Turn chop over. Cover with jam mixture using a knife. Reheat for 1 minute.

Sausage and Egg

1 pork sausage
1 egg
½ capsicum
1 cooked potato (optional)

Prick sausage skin in several places and arrange on a serving plate. Cook for 2 minutes. Break egg onto plate beside sausage. Prick yolk and white.

Cut capsicum and potato into thin slivers and arrange around egg on edge of plate. Cook for 2½ minutes. This gives a fairly soft egg.

Crème de Menthe Lamb

1 slice roast lamb
1 liqueur glass crème de menthe
1 liqueur glass water
1 teaspoon lemon juice

Marinate lamb in liquids for 15 minutes in small glass bowl. Cook for 2 minutes or until volume of liquid is slightly reduced.

Lamb with Mushrooms

2 lamb chops
1 can mushrooms in butter sauce
1 can French Onion soup
½ cup water

Add water to soup and mix well. Stir in mushrooms. Place lamb chops on serving dish and cover with sauce. Cook for 3 minutes or until well done.

Apricot Lamb

1 lamb chop
1 tablespoon apricot jam

Place lamb chop on a serving dish and cover with apricot jam. Cook for 2 minutes.

Mediterranean Lamb

1 cup diced, cooked lamb
1 jar cooked Ratatouille (see recipe
    under VEGETABLES)
black olives and dill for garnish

Place lamb in small glass bowl and cook on low for 3 minutes. Spoon ratatouille over and cook on high for a further 3 minutes. Garnish with black olives and dill.

Mediterranean Lamb

EGGS

Care must be taken when cooking eggs.
Remember to pierce both the yolk and white since
each cooks at a different speed. A toothpick is a
handy tool for piercing eggs. A beginner should
not try cooking them in the shell as they may
burst and splatter all over the oven. Always
slightly undercook eggs and let them stand for a
few minutes to finish off.

Fried Eggs

2 eggs
½ teaspoon unsalted butter

Melt butter on bread and butter plate for 30 seconds. Break eggs onto plate. Pierce yolks. Cook for 1 minute 20 seconds then let stand to set.

Poached Egg

1 egg
1 cup hot water

Boil water in medium-sized glass bowl. Break egg carefully into water so as to keep yolk intact. Cook on low for 4–4½ minutes.
   Note: Do not use metallic egg poachers.

Curried Eggs

1 clove garlic, crushed
½ teaspoon curry powder
1 teaspoon ghee
2 tablespoons tomato purée
1 slice lemon
1 teaspoon apricot jam
2 eggs
¼ cup milk

Combine garlic, curry powder and ghee in a cup and cook for 30 seconds. Add tomato purée, lemon and jam. Mix well and cook for 1 minute.
   Beat together eggs and milk in a glass bowl. Stir in all other ingredients.
   Cook on low for 5 minutes until egg is beginning to set. Stir with a fork to break up egg mass then cook for 2 minutes on high.

Scrambled Eggs

2 eggs
2 tablespoons cream or milk
1 tablespoon unsalted butter

Melt butter in ramekin for 30 seconds. Stir remaining ingredients together and pour into ramekin. Cook for 30 seconds. Stir. Cook for 1½ minutes then stir agin.
  Variation: Add a little chopped dill or parsley to the egg mixture before cooking.

Step 1: Melt 1 tablespoon unsalted butter in ramekin

Step 2: Mix eggs and cream together

Step 3: Pour egg mixture into ramekin and cook 2 minutes stirring twice during cooking time

Baked Custard

1 egg
¾ cup milk
pinch cinnamon

Break egg into coffee mug. Beat with fork then stir in milk. Mix well. Sprinkle top with cinnamon.
  Cook for 1½ minutes. Let stand for a further minute. Cook for 1½ minutes on low and watch carefully. Turn off immediately if mixture starts to boil.

'Haven't a Thing to Eat' Dessert

2 slices wholemeal bread
  (wholegrain is best)
1 egg
½ cup milk
½ small can diced pineapple,
  drained
1 jar cooked apple baby food
2 tablespoons white wine
½ teaspoon nutmeg

Arrange bread in bottom of a casserole dish. Beat egg and milk together and pour over bread. Cook for 2 minutes until custard is absorbed into the bread.
  Place pineapple on bread and cover with apple. Drench with wine, sprinkle with nutmeg and cook for 2½ minutes.

Bread and Butter Pudding

3 slices stale white bread
2 tablespoons unsalted butter
1 cup dried fruit, pre–soaked in
  wine
1 egg
¾ coffee mug milk
½ teaspoon cinnamon
½ teaspoon grated lemon rind
1 teaspoon grated root ginger

Wipe over the inside surface of a casserole dish with butter and spread butter on both surfaces of each slice of bread. Arrange bread slices over the bottom of the dish and cover with dried fruit.
  Beat egg in a coffee mug and add milk. Beat well. Add cinnamon and lemon rind and cook for 2 minutes.
  Pour custard over bread mixture so that liquid is absorbed by the bread. Sprinkle with ginger. Cook on low for 5 minutes or until set.

Scrambled Eggs

SNACKS

Many of the recipes in this section are substantial enough to serve as light meals.

When a cheese topping is called for do not cook for too long or the cheese will become rubbery and tough.

Penjas

3 thick slices liverwurst sausage
1 onion, chopped
1 can diced capsicum
½ cup cooked, diced vegetables
1 tomato
½ cup grated Parmesan cheese

Line base of ramekin or small soup plate with liverwurst sausage. Cover with chopped onion and dice capsicum, then vegetables, then thickly sliced tomato.

Sprinkle with Parmesan cheese and cook for 2–3 minutes, or until cheese has begun to melt.

Pâté

200 g liverwurst sausage
1 tablespoon unsalted butter
¼ teaspoon dried oregano
1 tablespoon Cognac

Mash sausage, butter and oregano together. Place in small glass bowl and cook for 2½ minutes. Remove, pour Cognac over pâté and let stand until cool.

White Elephant

2 slices rye bread
2 slices wholemeal or kibble bread
2 tablespoons pâté (see recipe
    above)
100 g ricotta cheese
1 can sweet corn, drained
1 medium-sized dill pickle, sliced
1 pickled or cocktail onion

Spread the 4 slices of bread with pâté. Cover slices 1 and 3 with corn and dill pickle. Cover slice 2 with ricotta cheese and pickled onion cut in half.

Heat each slice for 2 minutes. Stack bread slices so that outer 2 layers of filling are corn and centre one is cheese.

Pâté

Jamaican Toast

2 slices wholemeal or kibble bread
sweet chutney
2 slices ham
1 banana
½ onion, chopped
1 dill pickle or gherkin, sliced
several slices mozzarella cheese or
    more if required
sour cream, paprika and dill for
    garnish

Spread each slice of bread with chutney and cover with ham. Arrange slices of banana on each, then onion and dill pickle. Cover with mozzarella cheese.

Cook for 2 or 3 minutes until cheese has melted and is bubbling. Garnish with a dollop of sour cream sprinkled with paprika and a spray of dill.

Step 1: Spread chutney on bread and cover with ham

Step 2: Add banana, onion and dill pickle

Step 3: Cover with Mozzarella cheese and cook until cheese is bubbling

Danish Delight

1 ham steak or 1 thick sliced
    canned ham
1 onion, chopped
1 tablespoon vinegar
½ cup apricot nectar
1 teaspoon cooking oil

Heat oil in a glass jar for 30 seconds. Add chopped onion, vinegar and apricot nectar. Cook on low for 2 minutes. Let stand.

Arrange ham on serving plate. Cover with sauce and cook for further 2 minutes.

Sardine Potatoes

1 cup cooked mashed potato
½ can sardines, drained

Mix both ingredients with a fork in a glass jar. Cook for 2 minutes. Stir well and cook a further 1½ minutes.

Late Night Special

½ cup cooked potato (or potato
    salad)
½ can Cream of Celery soup
¼ cup grated cheese
2 slices toast

Mix together potato and soup in a ramekin. Sprinkle cheese over top. Heat for 2 minutes, or until cheese begins to melt. Pile the mixture on toast while hot.

Stuffed Mushrooms

4 large fresh mushrooms, washed
1 medium–sized dill pickle
2 shallots
3 tablespoons ricotta cheese

Wash mushrooms and remove stalks. Chop pickle, mushroom stalks and shallots and mix with ricotta cheese.

Stuff mixture into inverted mushroom caps and cook for 2 minutes. Serve with sliced fresh fruit.

Variation: Finely diced ham and red capsicum may be added to the mushroom stuffing.

Step 1: Wash mushrooms and remove stalks. Chop stalks, pickle and shallots

Step 2: Mix chopped ingredients with Ricotta cheese

Step 3: Stuff mixture into inverted mushroom caps

Winter Hearty

½ can peeled tomatoes
2 canned frankfurts, drained and
    chopped
½ can Pea and Ham soup

Stir tomatoes and frankfurts into soup. Cook in medium–sized glass bowl for 3 minutes.

French Collation

½ red or green capsicum, seeded
    and cut into strips
1 hard–boiled egg
½ can anchovy fillets
mayonnaise
bread roll

Chop egg and mix with anchovies, capsicum, and mayonnaise. Cook for 1½ minutes. Cut roll in half. Scoop bread out of crust and fill with mixture.

Empty Cupboard Surprise

1 can sweet corn
1 cup any cooked vegetable (a
   mixture is best)
½ cup any chopped, leftover meat
   (optional)
1 egg

Drain sweet corn and mix with vegetables and meat. Place in small glass bowl and break egg on top, piercing yolk with toothpick.
   Cook for 3 minutes or until egg is set. Cover and let stand for 2 minutes before eating.

Prince's Pocket

1 small wholemeal pita (pocket or
   Lebanese) bread
1 small can mushrooms in butter
   sauce
small handful walnuts, chopped
1 tomato, thinly sliced
chicken leftovers

Mix mushrooms, chicken, tomato and walnuts and cook for 2 minutes. Fill pita bread with mixture. Reheat on low heat for 2 minutes (optional).

Asparagus Snack

1 egg
½ cup milk
1 teaspoon grated lemon rind
½ can asparagus spears, drained
2 slices bread

Beat egg and milk together. Add lemon rind.
   Arrange bread on a dinner plate and place half the asparagus on each slice. Pour custard mixture over asparagus so it soaks into the bread.
   Cook for 2½ minutes.

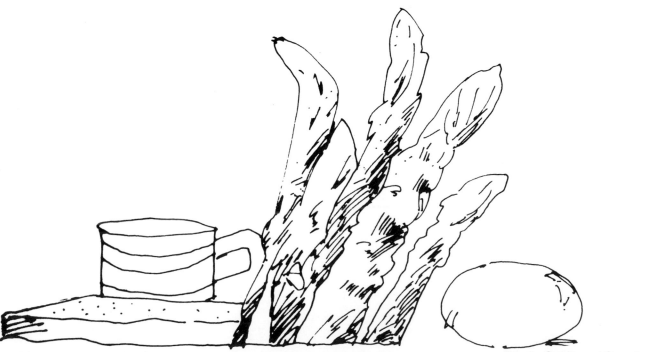

Empty Cupboard Surprise

Mediterranean Medley

⅓ cup Sun Gold Vita Rice
1 can tomatoes, drained
few olives (optional)
handful of raisins
1 clove garlic, crushed
½ cup grated Parmesan cheese
chopped fresh basil for garnish

Add equal quantity of boiling water to rice in bowl large enough to allow rice to swell. Put aside for 40 minutes. When rice is soft mix all ingredients together.

Cook on low for 5 minutes or until rice is tender. Garnish with basil.

Artichoke Hearts

1 can artichoke hearts
2 tablespoons unsalted butter
1 tablespoon vinegar
1 teaspoon horseradish

Heat butter with vinegar for 30 seconds in a glass jar. Add horseradish and mix well.

Arrange artichoke hearts on serving plate. Pour sauce on to each heart and cook for 2 minutes.

Corn on the Cob

1 fresh corn cob
1 tablespoon unsalted butter
pinch nutmeg

Remove silk from cob and place on serving dish. Dot corn with butter and cover with husks. Place on paper towel, double thickness.

Cook for 4 minutes. Allow to cool slightly before eating.

Silver Beet Parcels

3 silver beet or spinach leaves
1 cup cooled mashed pumpkin
¼ cup chopped chives or parsley
1 egg

Wash and drain leaves and remove white stalks. (Keep stalks for soup or a leftover dish.) Arrange each leaf flat on a dinner plate and heat for 30 seconds until tender.

Combine pumpkin, chives and egg. Mix well. Spoon pumpkin mixture onto centre of each leaf. Fold edges of silver beet over filling and roll up securely.

Arrange parcels on dinner plate and cook for 2½ minutes or until heated through.

Complete Meal Casserole

1 potato
1 parsnip
1 small carrot
¼ small cabbage
1 small choko (optional)
1 tablespoon Parmesan cheese
½ cup leftover roast beef pieces
¼ teaspoon caraway seeds

Peel potato and cut into quarters. Slice parsnip, carrot and choko (if used) thickly. Shred cabbage and mix in caraway seeds.

Combine all above ingredients in a casserole dish and cook for 3 minutes. Top with cheese and cook 1½ minutes more.

Vegetable Soup

½ can Celery soup
½ soup can water
1 stalk celery, chopped
½ cup frozen lima beans
½ cup frozen broccoli, broken into
   florets
1 zucchini, chopped
½ cup chopped white meat

Combine all ingredients in a large bowl. Cover with greaseproof paper and cook for 2½ minutes.

Salmon with Horseradish

1 can salmon, drained
1 tablespoon horseradish
2 small dill pickles, halved

Empty salmon on to plate. Break into several smaller chunks.

Add horseradish and arrange dill pickles around salmon. Cook for 2 minutes.

Complete Meal Casserole

Paella

½ cup cooked rice
½ onion, chopped
½ small can prawns or a few
   fresh green prawns, shelled
½ cup any cooked, diced fish
1 tomato
½ cup white wine
pinch oregano

Combine first 4 ingredients and place in a large glass mixing bowl. Pour over wine.

Slice tomato and arrange on top of rice mixture. Sprinkle with oregano. Cook on low for 3 minutes.

Variation: To give this dish the full Spanish treatment colour the rice with saffron and add some fresh peas.

Garlic Bread

1 long bread roll
60 g unsalted butter
1 clove garlic, crushed

Cut roll into about 5 slices. The ends need to be thicker than other pieces. Melt butter in a cup for 30 seconds. Mix garlic with butter.

Spread garlic butter on both sides of each slice. Form slices into roll and wrap tightly with greaseproof paper, tucking the ends well under. Cook for 2 minutes.

Paella

Hot Mash Potato Snack

2 medium-sized cooked potatoes
1 egg
1 tablespoon milk
½ cup chopped onion
1 tablespoon chutney
2–3 thick slices salami or 3
    Cheerios, chopped

Mash potato with egg and milk until smooth. Cook onion in a saucer for 50 seconds. Mix onion with chutney.

Arrange sausage and potato on serving plate and spoon chutney mixture over. Cook for 3 minutes.

Scallop Chowder Deluxe

1 can Scallop Chowder
1 chowder can water
½ cup frozen prawns
1 small can creamed corn
2 tablespoons sherry

Place scallop chowder and water in a large glass bowl and mix well. Cook for 3 minutes. Add other ingredients and cook for further 3 minutes.

This will make 2 hearty suppers. Freeze half until required.

Quick Casserole

1 can Celery soup
¼ cup grated Parmesan cheese
1 egg
1 slice stale bread, broken into
    small pieces
1 small can salmon or tuna

Heat soup in a casserole dish for 1 minute. Add cheese and heat for 30 seconds or until melted.

Combine with remaining ingredients and mix well. Cook for 3 minutes.

Baked Beans

1 small can baked beans
1 small can diced capsicum
¼ teaspoon curry powder
1 tablespoon Tomato Magic

Empty baked beans into mixing bowl. Drain capsicum, retaining liquid.

Mix Tomato Magic with 2 tablespoons of this liquid until dissolved. Add curry powder.

Combine all ingredients, cover with greaseproof paper and heat for 1½ minutes.

IMPORTANT QUESTIONS AND ANSWERS ABOUT FOOD

Eating alone should never be merely functional. Food is meant to be enjoyed. Set an attractive place for yourself as if you were a valued guest. Sit down to eat and take your time.

Why is it necessary to eat some raw food?

Plan your meal so that you eat some fresh raw food every day, preferably at every meal. For example, if you have porridge for breakfast also have an apple or orange. If for dinner you choose Pork and Bitters then finish off with fresh pineapple.

Raw foods contain no additives and no extra salt or sugar — remember, convenience foods may be high in these — and so help to keep your average daily intake of these things down.

Some nutrients are heat sensitive and are destroyed by cooking. However if food is microwaved correctly losses should be minimal.

You need raw foods to chew on to massage gums. Cooked foods are softer and don't provide much dental exercise.

How much salt can I eat?

Many foods naturally contain salt but these are not a problem. Excess salt in our diet increases the risk of hypertension. Some people seem to be more sensitive to a high salt intake than others; it is not known why. One teaspoon or 5 grams of salt is the recommended daily limit. Foods high in salt include canned and smoked fish, all canned savoury products, commercial sauces and dressings and take-away foods.

So when you eat foods high in salt, limit your intake and accompany them with fresh vegetables with no added salt.

What's so special about the cabbage family?

This family, which includes cabbage, cauliflower, broccoli and brussel sprouts, is strongly linked to a lowered incidence of stomach, colon and rectal cancers. So make sure you have substantial servings of these, preferably a few times each week.

Should I eat a white, yellow and green vegetable the way my mother taught me?

Mother was right. Each group of vegetables provides different nutrients. Yellow vegetables are high in carotene which is converted to vitamin A in the body. Vitamin A has also been linked with low incidence of some types of cancers. This book contains a number of recipes using yellow vegetables and fruits particularly carrots, pumpkins, pawpaw and mango. All yellow and green fruits and vegetables contain some carotene.

Green vegetables help to regulate your appetite, your bowel functions and your triglycerides (a group of fatty acids) and cholesterol level. Vegetables, fruits and cereals contain no cholesterol. But watch what you add to them. Added milk, cream and butter should be omitted if you have high triglycerides.

Why can't I just eat anything and swallow vitamin pills?

Unfortunately (or fortunately) we have developed physiological processes and controls based on bulky foods rather than on little pink pills. Good nutrition through a healthy diet seems to maximise our chances of good health. There is strong evidence of beneficial interactions between various food components. For example, high fibre vegetables increase the bulk of food mass and regulate its passage through the gastro-intestinal tract. Not all the nutrients in everything we eat are absorbed by the body. If food passes quickly, less nutrients are absorbed. Fats and cholesterol may be physically absorbed by the fibre and therefore just pass through. The rate of passage will also regulate the vitamins and minerals available for absorption. Little pink pills don't produce this type of good physiological balance and control.

Should I add lecithin to my breakfast cereal?

The body makes its own lecithin and a deficiency of lecithin has never been identified. It is a fat which occurs widely in both animal and plant foods. Eggs are a good source. Many extravagant claims have been made about it but a good balanced diet with plenty of variety will ensure you have an adequate lecithin intake.

Does garlic thin the blood?

Garlic, onions and other members of that family contain sulphur compounds which give them their characteristic smell. There is some evidence that these compounds do in fact lower blood fat levels preventing and retarding arteriosclerosis. Blood which is high in fat looks thick and milky.

Is bread fattening?

Both wholemeal and white bread are good food. Of course, an excess of any food is not desirable. If you are still a bit hungry after you've eaten your meat and vegetables, have some bread. Don't forget to vary the type of bread you buy. Bread is a good source of protein and thiamine (vitamin B$_1$) as well as other nutrients. But watch how much fat you add. Most breads are tasty without butter or margarine. If you are out of potatoes place a slice of bread on a plate and cover with meat or a chop. When you microwave this any juices from the meat will soak into the bread. It is delicious.

Is margarine better than butter?

Both should only be used sparingly. Margarine manufacture involves the addition of salt, flavouring and colouring. Although margarines with a low salt content are available, the levels are not as low as in unsalted butter. Hence the recommendation in this book to use butter. But excess of any one type of fat is undesirable. Use polyunsaturated oils when making up your own French dressing. Gram for gram, all fats, be they solid or liquid, have the same energy value (calories/kilojoules).

Should I eliminate potatoes from my diet?

Certainly not. A microwave potato in its jacket is a nutritious and substantial food. Two or three such potatoes are nutritionally superior to a packet of potato or corn chips or French fries.

What about eggs?

Eggs are an excellent source of protein and nearly all the other nutrients. They are grossly underrated and the cholesterol scare has given them something of a bad name. Only eat one egg on any particular day, preferably with bread and vegetables such as tomato, onion or spinach. Eggs are an excellent snack food and combine well with almost any leftovers.

How much meat can I eat?

In moderation, all types of meat form an important part of our diet. Meat is the chief source of iron for many Australians and is an excellent source of protein, niacin (vitamin B$_3$), vitamin A and many other nutrients. The problem is that meat can be very fatty and if you like a decent helping your fat intake could be high. Lot fed beef may contain fat between the muscle fibres which you don't see. Selvage fat, as occurs in lamb, is not a problem because you can easily see it and cut it off if you wish.

If you choose not to eat meat, then you MUST complement your vegetable protein and should seek advice from a competent dietitian.

People now seem to be eating less meat than previously, partly for health reasons and partly because they don't know what to do with some of the cuts. This book only uses cuts of meat which are easily identified even by the novice. But do experiment. Different cuts have different textures and tastes and can be rewarding to try.

Your plate should contain two thirds vegetables and one third meat.

In summary

You are probably eating a nutritionally sound diet if you are:

● not gaining or losing weight
● eating food from each of the food groups every day
● eating some raw food, preferably at each meal
● watching your salt intake
● watching your fat intake
● drinking fluid in the form of tea or coffee, water, soups or fruit juices etc. (not alcohol)
● watching your sugar intake
● a prudent shopper
● checking your fridge and pantry regularly and restocking when necessary.

COOKING CONTAINERS AND GADGETS

What to hoard

Save and hoard glass jars for cooking, and glass stoppered bottles for storage.

What to buy

Plates
Either ceramic which are specified 'suitable for microwave ovens' or cheap glass, paper or wood. Almost any plate will do, although it may get hot, depending on its composition.

Jars
Collect Vegemite and jam jars or any others with wide necks. To store leftovers, use glass jars with screw tops. These can also be used for cooking. *Never* use wide bodied jars with narrow necks. These are potential bombs. Labels on glass containers are sometimes made of foil. These must be removed as they prevent penetration of microwaves to the food.

Electric can opener
You are going to be opening many cans and can do without the constant hunt for a prehistoric monster which will cut your hands and fingers.

Funnel
Plastic or glass. Use for pouring — it will save endless accidents.

Colander
Useful for draining and shaking dry washed vegetables, also for draining contents of cans.

Ramekins and small casserole dishes
These are useful for soups.

Oven bags and elastic bands
For cooking a mixture of ingredients without mess. No washing up.

Greaseproof paper
To cover food which may splatter.

Steel knives and scissors
The self sharpening ones are useful and easy to find. Scissors to open packets should be kept close by.

Mugs
Good quality ones such as Wedgwood will state 'safe for microwave ovens'. These will not be hot to hold. Plastic ones are unsuitable.

Cups
Glass or ceramic. Beware of metal trims.

Glass bowls
Useful for cooking in and eating from. A small one is essential but a medium–sized one will also be useful. Buy a set of 3 of varying sizes. This will cover most cooking requirements.

Glass measuring jug
Two–cup size for measuring ingredients while getting used to amounts required for one.

SHOPPING

Important tips

When you go shopping, remember there is only one of you. Your stomach has only a limited capacity and fresh food is prone to spoilage, so buy small quantities. The bulk buying store is not for you. Don't buy foods prepacked and discounted. You are looking for good quality foods in small amounts.

Don't buy by weight — this can be misleading. Choose by number. You need two lamb chops, six potatoes, two tomatoes, four oranges and a handful of mushrooms. You don't need a whole cabbage, a five kilogram bag of potatoes or a whole watermelon! Enterprising shopkeepers are now selling wedges of watermelon, packs of shredded cabbage or coleslaw mix and packs of root vegetables for soup.

Some gourmet delicatessens sell cooked turkey and roast beef by the slice. They will also sell cheeses in the small amounts you want as well as small quantities of sausage and pâté. Find one near where you work or where you live.

Bread can be a major staple for the loner, so make it interesting. Don't buy a giant, economy-sized sandwich pack unless you eat sandwiches consistently every day. Try other varieties of bread — from dark pumpernickel to a light, white French loaf. They may be more expensive but you will have a variety of fresh bread more often. French bread is particularly delicious when fresh, but like most other breads freezes well and can be reheated straight from the freezer.

Shopping should not be a chore. Do all your shopping at no more than three shops. Initially, in a new district it may take time to find the right shops, but after that it is just a matter of a weekly visit with your shopping list.

Consult your diary before going shopping. Will you be having dinner at home every night? Will you be home over the weekend? Do you expect visitors? Shop accordingly. Don't buy up fresh food if you are likely to be away. Perhaps get a few apples to keep in the fridge. They will keep for well over a week and you'll have some fresh fruit when you return. Remember, after you've been away you may not have time for a major shopping spree for a few days. So check pantry and freezer stocks.

Beware of lot fed beef. It may taste well and be tender, but that is due to its high fat content, a result of cereal feeding. The grass fed free range animal is tougher but better for your health. Ask for identification of the meat you buy. Hogget is one year old lamb. Cheap hogget may turn out to be expensive mutton, so again beware and be a discriminating consumer. If the meat is tough and fatty, it's probably mutton and should go into a stew.

Your shopping list

From the supermarket

Bread, dry biscuits or crispbread
Breakfast cereal — preferably Weet-bix, Vita-brits, Weeties or Puffed Rice, oatmeal, first break wheat or wholemeal, semolina
Rice — Sun Gold Vita Rice is best, but any white rice will do
Fresh or frozen corn cobs
Sardines or sprats
Canned salmon or tuna
Frozen fish pieces
Frozen prawns
Tomato paste — small, preferably in glass jar. Buy two small jars rather than one large jar or it may go mouldy
Tomato Magic — not synthetic
Canned tomatoes — house brand
Canned soups — Celery, French Onion, Lobster Bisque, Cream of Mushroom
Canned mushrooms in butter — buy Australian
Baked beans
Canned kidney beans or Three Bean Mix
Canned diced capsicum — small can
Canned asparagus spears
Canned beetroot
Sauerkraut — if you like it
Unsalted butter
Half dozen eggs
Vinegar — white, in glass bottle preferably. If in plastic, transfer to glass bottle to store at home
Apricot nectar — usually with the fruit drinks
Crystallised ginger
Sultanas — buy a large pack. Eat by the handful when hungry if you are not counting kilojoules
Canned fruit — three favourite varieties in small cans, canned in water or natural juice
Vegemite
Long life milk (UHT milk) — a nutritionally sound choice
Frozen apple pie
Almonds and walnuts — small packets of chopped nuts
Jam — apricot and plum. Continental varieties in glass jars containing a lot of fruit are available from delicatessens
Ice cream — make sure the words 'ice cream' are on the label
Herbs and spices — black peppercorns, dried basil, oregano, cumin, coriander, cinnamon, nutmeg, ginger
Frozen veges — peas or beans, cauliflower or broccoli, brussel sprouts

From your friendly delicatessen

Salad oil — buy either Spanish olive oil or cold pressed walnut, sunflower or other vegetable oil. Buy smallest quantity available

Maple syrup — best Canadian is essential to pour over your canned fruit or ice cream. Contains fructose so only a small amount is required even if you love sweet food

Dijon mustard — buy the one in the earthenware container. Genuine French is best. Beware of 'Dijon style'

Horseradish — grated, in a bottle is the best choice

Curry paste — Bolst is readily available. Curried tuna on toast is a nutritious weekend snack

Cheese — depends on what you like. Most delis give you a bit to try. The one full of dried apricots makes a wonderful dessert. The harder and more mature the cheese the longer it keeps

Sausage — Plumrose Cheerios in a can. Hungarian or Budapest salami is expensive, but worth it

Ham — ask for a slice or two from the bone

Artichoke hearts — Spanish or Italian in glass bottles are the best and they'll keep after the bottle has been opened

Hearts of palms — usually in cans, but not always available. The universal appetiser

Macadamia nuts — Planters are vacuum packed and will keep for ages unopened

From the corner street stall or your favourite aunt

Chutney — mango is best. Also available from the deli

Pickles — cauliflower and carrot

Jams — strawberry, rosella or cumquat marmalade

COLD STORAGE

The fridge

The refrigerator is one of the most abused and underused pieces of kitchen equipment. It should never be bare, but it must be kept clean and free of smells. If foods are stored correctly and normal care is taken, a frost free refrigerator rarely needs total cleaning.

Keep clean, empty glass jars for storing unused portions of canned soups, gravies and leftovers. The jars can then be transferred straight to the microwave oven for reheating.

A guide for food storage:

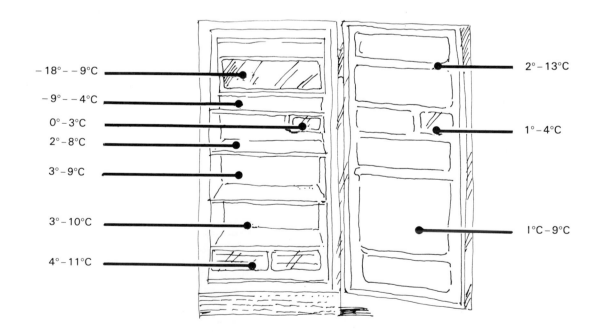

- -18°--9°C
- -9°--4°C
- 0°-3°C
- 2°-8°C
- 3°-9°C
- 3°-10°C
- 4°-11°C
- 2°-13°C
- 1°-4°C
- 1°C-9°C

Food type	Storage temperature °C	Shelf life in the home
Seafoods	0–3	3 days
Crustaceans, molluscs	0–3	2 days
Meat	0–3	3–5 days
Minced meat, offal	0–3	2–3 days
Cured meat	0–3	3 days
Poultry	0–7	3 days
Fruit juices	0–7	7–14 days
Milk	1–7	5–7 days
Cream	1–7	5 days
Cheese	0–7	variable (1–3 mths)
Butter	0–7	8 weeks
Oil, fat	2–7	variable (6 mths)
Margarine	2–7	variable (6 mths)

Wrapped fresh meat can be kept for up to 3–5 days at 0°–3°C, i.e. in the meat compartment of the average domestic refrigerator. If you think you may not consume it in that time, remove the shop wrapping, place in a plastic bag, label with contents and date and place in the freezer.

Store animal protein foods in the highest, coldest part of the fridge. Cover all cooked food and foods with strong odours. According to the C.S.I.R.O. Division of Food Research, closed glass or plastic containers are preferable to the common cling wrap polyethylene films. The larger a piece of meat, the longer will be its keeping time.

The freezer

Despite various sources of conventional wisdom, a person living alone doesn't need a freezer stuffed full of food. But it's a nice luxury to have. Before food is placed in the freezer the package should be clearly labelled in felt pen with the date.

According to the C.S.I.R.O., if the whole package is not to be consumed completely at one meal, the unwanted portion should be re-wrapped, placed in a plastic bag and returned to the freezer immediately. Generally speaking, thawed food should not be re-frozen.

Storage times for frozen foods:

Food type	Recommended maximum storage time in the home freezer (months)
Bacon (smoked)	1–2
Beef (uncooked)	6
Bread, baked	2
Chicken (uncooked)	6
Concentrated fruit juices	6
Cooked, spiced dishes	2
Crab	3
Crayfish	3
Fish	3–4
French fried potatoes	6
Fruit	6
Green vegetables	6

THE PANTRY

Use of canned foods

Canned foods are sterilised by heating during manufacture and the can prevents recontamination during storage and transport. Bacterial spoilage therefore does not occur with properly processed canned products.

Slow chemical changes do however take place in the cans, so the food has a long, but not an indefinite, storage life. Storage life depends on several factors but especially on the nature of the food and the conditions of storage. Always store cans in a cool, dry cupboard.

You should read the label carefully either at the time of purchase or before storing. The date of purchase should be marked on the can if extended storage is likely. Certain canned products, e.g. some canned hams and some imported fish products, must be refrigerated at all times. This requirement will be stated on the label and such cans should only be bought if they are displayed in a chilled cabinet in the retail store.

Don't buy or open canned foods if the cans show signs of swelling or leakage or have more than a small amount of external rusting. Do not buy dented cans.

A turnover of canned foods in your pantry about once a year is recommended. There is no sudden change from acceptability to unacceptability. However, changes in colour, texture or flavour slowly develop to the point where the food is no longer as pleasant to eat as it might be. The vitamin content of canned food also decreases slowly even when the cans are stored in cool conditions.

Freshly opened canned food should be treated as though it was recently cooked in the home. If not eaten at one meal it should always be refrigerated. Some foods, when stored in the opened can, dissolve tin and iron from the can slowly and the food may develop a metallic taste. The dissolved metal is not harmful but these foods, especially fruit, fruit juices and tomato products, should preferably be placed in a clean plastic or glass container and refrigerated. Adopt this practice for all canned foods.

Use of dried foods

Dried foods undergo slow chemical changes which lead to gradual loss of quality. These changes are accelerated by high temperature and exposure to air — particularly humid air.

Storage times set down in the table apply to foods stored under cool and dry conditions. The recommended maximum storage times in the home are for foods in unopened containers. After the original container is opened any unused portion should be transferred to a screw-top jar, sealable metal container or air-tight plastic container.

The main problem with dried foods is caused by insect infestation; regular inspection — at least once a fortnight — is recommended. Eggs laid by insects in the foodstuff before packaging may survive fumigation treatment, and under warm and moist conditions will hatch grubs and moths or weevils. Insects may also get into dried foods after the package is opened at home or even by making entry holes into some packages. Insect-infested food is not unsafe to eat but is usually rejected on aesthetic grounds. The likelihood of insect attack is a strong argument against the home storage of large quantities of dried food.

You should not eat foods showing mould growth, as they may be toxic. Mould growth should not occur unless dried foods have absorbed excessive moisture.

Take note of the 'use by' date. Look, smell and prod the food (in that order) after the expiry date. Don't automatically discard.

Dehydrated or dried food — storage times:

Food type	Recommended maximum storage time in the home in unopened containers
Beverages	
tea	3 mths
coffee, instant	3 mths
coffee, ground	3 mths
Biscuits	
savoury	6 wks
sweet	6 wks
Breakfast cereals	2 mths
Uncooked breakfast	
cereals eg oats	2 mths
Chocolate	
dark	3 mths
milk	3 mths
speciality	3 mths
Milk, powdered	6 mths
Prunes	4 mths
Other dried fruits	8 mths
Glace fruits	8 mths
Dried vegetables	6 mths
Flour	1 yr
Jelly crystals	8 mths
Pasta, eg spaghetti	6 mths
Polished rice	8 mths

Reproduced by permission from 'Storage Life of Foods' C.S.I.R.O., Division of Food Research.

INDEX